JAN 0 9

JAN 0 9

DIGGING INTO HISTORY

SOLVING THE MYSTERIES OF
AZTEC CITIES

Anita Croy

Marshall Cavendish
Benchmark
New York

Marshall Cavendish Benchmark
99 White Plains Road
Tarrytown, New York 10591
www.marshallcavendish.us

Library of Congress Cataloging-in-Publication Data

Croy, Anita.
Solving the mysteries of Aztec cities / by Anita Croy.
p. cm. -- (Digging into history)
Includes bibliographical references and index.
ISBN 978-0-7614-3102-2
1. Templo Mayor (Mexico City, Mexico)--Juvenile literature. 2. Aztec architecture--Mexico--Mexico City--Juvenile
literature. 3. Aztecs--Urban residence--Mexico--Mexico City--Juvenile literature. 4. Aztecs--Mexico--Mexico City--
Antiquities--Juvenile literature. 5. Excavations (Archaeology)--Mexico--Mexico City--Juvenile literature. 6. Mexico
City (Mexico)--Antiquities--Juvenile literature. I. Title.
F1219.1.M5C76 2009
972'.53--dc22
2008023056

Picture credits
Front Cover: Shutterstock: Gordon Galbraith

The photographs in this book are used by permission and through the courtesy of:
Alamy: Jon Arnold Images 5, Keith Dannemiller 14, David R. Frazier Photolibrary 28, Craig Lovell 17l, MJ Photography 25,
North Wind Pictures Archive 12, The Print Collector 6b, Mireille Vautier 21, 27, Visual Arts Library 18; **Art Archive:** Gianni
Dagli Orti 17r; **Bridgeman Art Library:** Biblioteca Nacional 1, 10, Museo Nacional de Antropologia 19; **Corbis:** Daniel
Aguilar 4-5, 6t, Morton Beebe 8, Bettmann 9, 20, 24, Gianni Dagli Orti 7, Marlo Guzman 26-27, Handout 29b, The Gallery
Collection 23, Robert van der Hilst 29t, Werner Forman 13, 15, 16; **Shutterstock:** Bill Perry 22, Ian D. Walker 11.

Marshall Cavendish Editor: Megan Comerford
Marshall Cavendish Publisher: Michelle Bisson

Series created by The Brown Reference Group plc
www.brownreference.com
Designer: Dave Allen
Picture Researcher: Clare Newman
Managing Editor: Tim Cooke
Indexer: Kay Ollerenshaw

Printed in China
1 3 5 6 4 2

Contents

WHAT LIES BENEATH THE CITY?

MEXICO CITY IS ONE OF THE WORLD'S BIGGEST CITIES—BUT BURIED BENEATH ITS STREETS ARE THE REMAINS OF ANOTHER URBAN CENTER.

In the heart of Mexico City, the capital of Mexico, stands one of the biggest squares in the world. The Zocalo was built by the Spanish **conquistadors** who settled in Mexico more than five hundred years ago. But what was there before the Spanish arrived? Clues started to emerge in the 1960s and 1970s. Workers digging a new subway system found ancient ruins beneath the city streets. Beside the Zocalo itself they found the ruins of an ancient temple. There we

stones carved with ancient figures and the **foundation** of a large building.

HEART OF THE EMPIRE

For Mexican archaeologist Eduardo Matos Moctezuma, this was an exciting moment. From old accounts left by the conquistadors, he believed that he had found the Templo Mayor, or Great Temple. It stood at the heart of the capital of the Aztec **Empire**, which dominated Mexico between 1430 and 1521. The Spanish invaders reported that the Aztec city, Tenochtitlán, was home to nearly 200,000 people. At the time, the biggest city at home in Spain had only 60,000 inhabitants.

AZTEC CAPITAL

Tenochtitlán stood on an island in a lake. It was joined to the lake shore by three wide causeways, or raised embankments. The Templo Mayor stood in a **sacred** area in the middle

LEFT: *Archaeologists excavate a wall at the Templo Mayor in Mexico City. Discoveries are being made all the time.*

ABOVE: *The Templo Mayor was near what is now Mexico City's main square, the Zocalo. The Spanish built a cathedral (left) and the National Palace (right) near the site.*

of the city. It was a huge **pyramid** that towered over the other buildings, topped with two smaller temples. The structures were coated with bright plaster: reds, greens, blues, and yellows. One was dedicated to Huitzilopochtli, the Aztec god of war. It was blood red. The other temple was dedicated to Tlaloc, the rain god. The conquistadors recorded that the Aztec used the temples to **sacrifice** prisoners they had captured in battle.

WARRIORS AND FARMERS

The gods of the temples show the nature of Aztec society. The Aztec were

RIGHT: *This stone carving of a face was one of fourteen discovered at the Templo Mayor site in Mexico City in January 2005.*

warriors. They rose to power by defeating their neighbors and taking their territory into the Aztec Empire. But the Aztec were also farmers. They worshipped the rain god because they depended on rain to grow crops.

CONTINUING DISCOVERIES

Since Matos Moctezuma began the first **excavations** at the Templo Mayor in the 1960s, the site has yielded more secrets. Experts have used computers to re-create how the temple was built. It was enlarged five times, probably by rulers who wanted to display their own glory. Evidence also shows that the Aztec had to make regular repairs. Although builders drove logs into the soft soil to make foundations for building, heavy stones tended to sink over time.

MORE TO COME

Work is still going on at the Templo Mayor. In 2006, excavators found a

LEFT: *This contemporary image shows Aztec warriors defending the Templo Mayor against Spanish attackers in 1521. The Spanish conquered the city—and the rest of the empire.*

huge carved stone. At more than 13 tons, it was the largest carved Aztec block ever discovered. Experts think that it may even hide a buried temple. No one knows for sure. It will take years to clear the stone and move it.

Such discoveries are slowly adding to our knowledge of Tenochtitlán. Finding out about the Aztec can be difficult, however. Most Aztec lived in cities and towns that were later built over by the Spanish. Relatively few sites have been excavated, so there is much more to learn about the ancient Aztec.

BELOW: *The Aztec said that Coyolxauhqui, carved into this round stone from the Templo Mayor, was an evil sorceress who spoke to centipedes and spiders.*

A Stone of Death

Near the foot of the pyramid in Templo Mayor, archaeologists found a large, round stone broken in two. When they put it back together, it displayed a grim carving: a female body cut into pieces.

The female was Coyolxauhqui, the sister of the god Huitzilopochtli and one of the founders of the Aztec. In an Aztec myth, the brother and sister had led the Aztec to Tenochtitlán. When they got there, the pair fought. The war god killed his sister and cut her into pieces.

The experts think that the bodies of sacrificial victims may have landed on the stone when they were rolled off the temple. It may have been a reminder to the Aztec that defeat and death were never far away.

Digging in the City

Archaeologists who study the Aztec have some tough problems. In Mexico City and other places, Aztec ruins now lie beneath newer buildings, making it difficult for archaeologists to study them. When Eduardo Matos Moctezuma started to excavate the Templo Mayor, he began digging in a parking lot. Later, he had to knock down modern buildings to get at other parts of the site. In many places, that is not possible. Authorities do not let archaeologists destroy people's homes or businesses.

?
DID YOU KNOW

The building of the Mexico City subway in the 1960s turned up so many Aztec artifacts that experts have not cataloged them all.

BELOW: *The foundations of the Templo Mayor stand in the heart of Mexico City.*

Save Our Past!

The National Institute of History and Anthropology in Mexico City has a special department ready to rescue **artifacts** that turn up during construction projects. The city government can also delay construction if workers discover ruins. That gives archaeologists a chance to study the site but usually not for long. They try to make careful records and remove any artifacts that might teach them more about the Aztec before the site is destroyed when building resumes.

ABOVE: *Workers complete the subway station at Pino Suárez around the base of an ancient Aztec temple.*

Sometimes it is possible to build around an ancient site. When a subway station was being constructed at Pino Suárez in Mexico City, for example, the builders found the remains of a round Aztec temple. The **architects** who designed the station came up with new plans. They left the temple on display, so that people could see it as they traveled to school or work.

WHO BUILT THE CITY?

HOW DID A SMALL GROUP OF NOMADIC FARMERS CREATE AN EMPIRE THAT COVERED MOST OF MODERN-DAY MEXICO?

When the Spanish arrived in Mexico in 1519, the Aztec ruled a huge empire. The Aztec told the European visitors a **myth** about the founding of Tenochtitlán. According to the myth, the Mexica, more commonly known as the Aztec, came from a dry, desert homeland to the north. The tribe wandered for generations before settling on the shore of a swampy lake named Texcoco in the middle of what is now

BELOW: *This codex illustration shows the construction of the Aztec capital, Tenochtitlán. The Aztec dated the founding of the city to 1325.*

Mexico. To escape attacks, the Aztec moved further into the swamp, where they found an eagle perched on a cactus. According to the myth, this was a sign from the god Huitzilopochtli. It showed the Aztec where to build a city. They called the place Tenochtitlán; the name means "place of the prickly pear cactus."

The Aztec recorded their history in books called codices (singular, **codex**). Scribes painted picture symbols called **glyphs** to stand for things such as dates, people, or cities. One codex dates the founding of Tenochtitlán to 1325.

FIGHT FOR POWER

The Aztec were surrounded by stronger tribes, such as the Colhuacan, Tenayuca, and Tepanec. They often fought. The Aztec became paid soldiers for the Tepanec. That gave them the chance to grow more powerful themselves. Eventually their warriors overthrew not only the Tepanec, but also the Colhuacan and the Tenayuca.

Every time the Aztec conquered another people, the defeated people and their territory became part of the Aztec Empire. They had to send gold and other valuable goods to Tenochtitlán as **tribute**. These goods made the Aztec

Before the Aztec

The Aztec were not the first people to rule an empire in Mexico. Two thousand years earlier, the Olmec built cities near what is now the Gulf of Mexico. They built the first city in the Americas, San Lorenzo, in about 1200 B.C.E. It was a ceremonial center for three centuries. Hundreds of years later, between 200 and 600 C.E., the city of Teotihuacan (below) flourished in central Mexico. The Aztec were awed by the abandoned city and believed the gods were born there. Teotihuacan is the Aztec word for "place of the gods." Archaeologists still don't know who built Teotihuacan or why it was abandoned.

even more powerful. So, too, did **alliances** with other peoples.

WHO WERE THE AZTEC?

Although Tenochtitlán was the heart of the empire, it was not the only city. Other cities also stood throughout what is now central Mexico. They were often the capitals of **city-states** conquered by the Aztec.

TRADING CENTER

On the shore of Lake Texcoco stood Tlatelolco. It was home to the Aztec's main marketplace. Merchants brought goods there from as far south as what is now Panama.

There was also trade within the Aztec Empire itself. At towns such as Yautepec, south of Tenochtitlán,

ABOVE: *The people of Tenochtitlán called themselves the Mexica. The term Aztec was first used in the eighteenth century. Today it is used to describe not just the Mexica, but all the peoples of the empire.*

excavators found broken spindles and looms that were used to spin and weave **textiles**. Experts believe that women wove cloth and then swapped it for supplies such as bronze, which could be made into tools and artifacts. Bronze came from western Mexico. Trade routes held the empire together.

SPECIAL ROLES

Some Aztec were not traders, farmers, or warriors. They had special roles in society. Healers used herbs to make cures. The Spanish noted that Aztec medicine was far more advanced than European medicine of the time. There were also artists who drew the codices, and artisans who made paper and paint. Priests, who had a privileged place in society, were required to help people worship the gods.

Outside the Cities

For a long time, experts in Aztec **archaeology** mainly studied Aztec cities. They were interested in temples and stone palaces. But most of the Aztec were not priests or rulers. They were farmers who lived outside the cities. In the 1960s, excavators grew more curious about how the majority of the Aztec lived. They investigated villages far from Tenochtitlán. At Capilco, for example, there were just twenty-one homes. The Tlahuica people who lived there were subjects of the Mexica.

They lived in small one-room homes made of mud bricks. Outside was a courtyard where people did their cooking. They threw their trash, including broken pottery, in heaps. The pottery is full of clues for archaeologists. It shows, for example, that the Aztec ate dishes similar to Mexican food, such as beans and tortillas, that is now popular around the world.

ABOVE: *Aztec pottery varied from highly crafted and decorated items like these to plain, coarser ware used for everyday purposes.*

WHAT WERE THE TEMPLES FOR?

THE EMPIRE WAS BASED ON HUMAN SACRIFICE, WHICH WAS ESSENTIAL TO MAKING SURE THAT THE GODS LOOKED AFTER THE AZTEC.

When Matos Moctezuma excavated the Templo Mayor in Mexico City, he made a chilling discovery. On top on the pyramid dedicated to the war god Huitzilopochtli was a small stone. Matos Moctezuma knew instantly what it was for. The Spanish who conquered the Aztec in the sixteenth century had described it. This was where Aztec priests killed their prisoners. A captive was led to the top of the pyramid. Four priests lay the prisoner on his or her

BELOW: *A researcher examines a skull found near the Templo Mayor. It has a sharp flint for a nose and bone plugs for its eyes, and may have been worn as a mask.*

back over the small stone and held his or her legs and arms. Another priest used a dagger to swiftly cut open the victim's chest and pull out his or her heart while it was still beating. Then the dead body was pushed off the top of the pyramid to roll down the steps.

BELOW: *This handle decorated with turquoise was attached to a sharp blade. It may have been used in ritual killings.*

EMPIRE OF SACRIFICE

The conquistadors recorded that thousands of prisoners were killed in great ceremonies. When they were fighting the Aztec for control of Tenochtitlán, the conquistadors even witnessed the execution of some of their own men who had been captured.

The Templo Mayor was at the heart of the Aztec system to keep the gods happy. The Aztec had a complicated calendar. It divided history into ages, each of which was ruled by a particular god. At the end of the age in which the Aztec lived, they believed that the world would be destroyed.

WARRIORS AND GODS

Aztec religion depended on a constant supply of victims for sacrifice. That required warriors to capture prisoners on

The Aztec Calendar

One of the first artifacts found at the Templo Mayor, in 1790, was a round stone 12 feet (3.7 m) across. It was carved with symbols of the Aztec calendar. The stone also showed how four previous worlds had ended in disaster: jaguars, hurricanes, volcanoes, and torrential rain. The fifth age, in which the Aztec lived, had begun in 986 C.E. The Aztec believed that it would be the last age of humankind.

the battlefield. Young Aztec men could be called into the army at age twenty. They were trained to take prisoners using clubs, bows and arrows, and slings. Once they had captured four enemy prisoners, they joined the band of elite warriors.

In return for their service, the warriors got rewarded with luxury goods from other places in the empire. The most valuable rewards of all, such as jade or jaguar skins, could not be bought: they could only be gotten as gifts from the king. The Aztec rulers

Warrior Sanctuary

At Malinalco, about 70 miles (113 km) southwest of Mexico City, archaeologists found a group of buildings carved into cliffs. The structures once stood near the edge of the Aztec empire. They include temples that were probably used for **rituals** by two elite military cults: the Eagle Knights and the Jaguar Knights. One circular temple has an entrance shaped like a serpent's mouth. Inside are carvings of eagles and jaguars. Warriors admitted to the cults enjoyed many privileges, such as not having to pay taxes.

could only get those goods by keeping control of their enemies or by remaining rich enough to buy them. As the empire grew, the Aztec rulers needed even more warriors to support it. But that meant that they had to keep conquering more people to ensure the supply of luxury goods. The empire had to keep growing to survive.

LEFT: *The Aztec believed that the most valuable gemstone was jade, as used in this mask.*

SIGNS OF PRIVILEGE

That was one reason that Tenochtitlán and Tlatelolco were so busy. In the market at Tlatelolco the Spanish were astonished by the range of goods for sale. They included colored cotton, paper, and paints, as well as food and pottery. There were also luxury goods such as green jade, jaguar skins, and colorful feathers. Such items could only be bought by the richest Aztec, including the warriors. They marked out anyone who wore them as part of the **elite**.

RIGHT: *These illustrations of two Aztec gods show them with feathers in their headdresses. One of the gods carries an object made from green jade.*

An Empire Dedicated to Death

The Spanish conquistadors were horrified by the spectacles they saw on top of the pyramids of the Templo Mayor in Tenochtitlán. Priests killed hundreds of human sacrifices by ripping out their hearts and then rolling the bodies down the steep steps. The hearts were placed in a carved stone basin as offerings to the god Huitzilopochtli.

Some scholars believe that the Aztec sacrificed as many as 20,000 people throughout the empire each year. Most of the victims were slaves or captives. Aztec warriors were encouraged to capture their enemies alive on the

?

DID YOU KNOW

Some Aztec slaves were chosen to represent gods or goddesses. They enjoyed great luxury for a year—but then they were sacrificed.

BELOW: *A victim is sacrificed on a pyramid in an illustration made by an Aztec artist for the Spanish.*

battlefield—and if possible without wounding them. An injured captive was not suitable to offer to the god.

ABOVE: *Battle scenes decorate a circular stone set up by a ruler named Tizoc to celebrate his success in taking captives to be sacrificed.*

WHY SACRIFICE?

The purpose of the sacrifices was partly religious. The Aztec believed that the war god needed constant offerings of human hearts and blood. Without them, Huitzilopochtli would grow weak and not be able to fight off the nighttime and make the sun rise again the next morning.

Some modern scholars, however, have reconsidered the role of sacrifice in Aztec society. They argue that it was also an important way of supporting the social structure. It made warriors vital to Aztec society to supply captives. That in turn helped the Aztec conquer their nearby city-states and demand tribute from them, which made Tenochtitlán wealthy. The system of sacrifice was therefore at the center of Aztec success.

Other experts argue that, in some ways, Aztec sacrifice was not very different from today. They say that warfare always has casualties. The Aztec simply killed their victims on the pyramids rather than on the battlefield.

WHAT BECAME OF THE AZTEC EMPIRE?

WITHIN A COUPLE OF YEARS OF THE SPANISH ARRIVING IN MEXICO IN 1519, THE MIGHTY AZTEC EMPIRE HAD BEEN OVERTHROWN. HOW DID IT FALL SO QUICKLY?

The conquistadors who arrived in the Aztec Empire in 1519 were searching for gold and other treasure. Their leader, Hernán Cortés, led a small group of just six hundred soldiers from the coast of the Gulf of Mexico to Tenochtitlán. Along the way, they met peoples who had been conquered by the Aztec. The subject peoples were happy to make alliances with the Spanish against their Aztec rulers.

RIGHT: *The Spanish brought sixteen horses with them to the New World. The Aztec had never seen such animals before. No horses existed in the Americas.*

CONQUERING THE CITY

In Tenochtitlán the conquistadors met the Aztec emperor, Moctezuma II. For a while the Aztec and the new arrivals got along. The Aztec soon became suspicious of the Spanish, however, who were only interested in gathering gold and other treasure. The Aztec wanted to drive the conquistadors from the city. The Spanish took Moctezuma captive. When crowds of Aztecs stoned the conquistadors, Moctezuma tried to calm his people. Violence flared, and Moctezuma was killed. The Spanish fled the city.

Ten months later, Cortés returned. This time he brought native warriors as allies. The Spanish killed nearly two-thirds of the city's population. They had guns and cannons, while the Aztec

LEFT: *This nineteenth-century image shows the first meeting of Cortés and Moctezuma.*

defenders had only spears, clubs, and slings. At the end of the seventy-five-day siege, the mighty capital lay in ruins. One Aztec poet wrote, "There is nothing but grief and suffering in Mexico [Tenochtitlan] and Tlatelolco, where once we saw beauty and valor."

WHO'S TELLING THE TRUTH?

Most contemporary descriptions of the Spanish conquest of the Aztec Empire were written by the Spanish. Historians have to be careful how they interpret the accounts. Some conquistadors made the Aztec sound as if they were violent and uncivilized. They were careful to justify everything the Spanish did. That means that their accounts may not be reliable. For example, most conquistadors reported that it was the Aztec themselves who stoned Moctezuma to death. However, other **chroniclers** noted that the emperor had been stabbed to death by the conquistadors holding him captive.

The Spanish tried to convert the Aztec

BELOW: *The Plaza of the Three Cultures in Mexico City marks the site of the final Aztec defeat. It combines Aztec and colonial Spanish ruins with the modern city.*

Heroine or Traitor?

ABOVE: *This contemporary Spanish illustration shows the Spanish ships arriving in Mexico and Marina acting as a translator.*

One of the most controversial figures from the story of the fall of the Aztec Empire is an Indian translator named Doña Marina. Marina was one of many slaves given to Hernán Cortés after he had defeated the Mexican state of Potonchan. She started translating the Aztec language, Nahuatl, into a Mayan language that one of the conquistadors could speak. Soon, she learned enough Spanish to translate directly from Nahuatl. She took part in **negotiations** between Moctezuma and Cortés. The Spanish said that they could never have conquered Tenochtitlán without the help of the translator. Later, Marina had Cortés's child. He was one of the first mestizos, people of both European and Aztec heritage.

For modern descendants of the Aztec, Marina is a symbol of treachery. They call her La Malinche, or "the stain," and argue that she betrayed her people.

ABOVE: *These Aztec artifacts, including pieces of pottery and statues, were found in Mexico City in 1970 during construction work on a subway line.*

to Christianity. The Catholic Church built churches on top of Aztec temples. It ordered statues to be destroyed. In the city of Cuernavaca, Cortés built himself a palace on top of an Aztec palace. Spanish settlers started to build on top of Tenochtitlán and other cities.

SYMPATHETIC SPANIARDS

Some of the Spanish were sympathetic toward the Aztec. They included monks such as Bernardino de Sahagún and Diego Durán, who learned to speak Nahuatl. Sahagún commissioned Aztec artists to produce new codices about their history and religion. He believed it would be easier to convert Aztecs to Christianity by first understanding their faith. Durán criticized Cortés. He said that the conquistador had committed "frightful and cruel atrocities" against the Aztec.

WEAKENED BY DISEASE

Neverthless, the Spanish government wanted to obliterate Aztec culture. The unintentional spread of disease helped the conquistadors achieve this goal. The Aztec had never been exposed to many of the diseases carried by the Spanish, so they had no natural defenses against them. Even diseases that were not often fatal in Europe, such as influenza, could kill people with no **immunity** against them. Infection spread quickly among the native peoples. Millions of Aztec may have died from diseases such as smallpox, weakening the empire.

TOOLS AND TECHNIQUES – TOOLS AND TECHNIQUES – TOOLS AND TECHNIQUES – TOOLS AND TECHNIQUES – TOOLS AND TECHNIQUES – TOOLS AND TECHNIQUES

Burying the City

Much of Tenochtitlán was destroyed in the long siege of the city. The conquistadors set fire to homes and pulled down statues in temples. They used stones from destroyed structures for their own buildings. The Catholic Church ordered the destruction of all traces of the Aztec pagan religion, such as temples or statues. The Spanish currency mint and the National Palace were built on the site of Moctezuma's palace. The Spanish also used rubble from Aztec buildings to fill in the canals that ran through the city. Eventually, they filled in or drained the water from Lake Texcoco.

BELOW: *This carving of a skull was excavated on the site of Tlatelolco.*

WHAT IS LEFT TO DISCOVER?

FOR DECADES, MOST RESEARCH ON THE AZTEC TOOK PLACE IN LIBRARIES. TODAY, NEW EXCAVATIONS ARE YIELDING MORE INFORMATION.

The Aztec are one of the most intriguing of all ancient peoples. Everyone is fascinated by the stories of mass sacrifices on top of the temple pyramids. People are also interested in learning how the Aztec built

such a huge empire—and how they managed to lose it so quickly to only a few hundred conquistadors. Archaeologists hope they will uncover details of the rise and fall of the Aztec.

NEW SOURCES OF INFORMATION

Experts have learned a lot about how the Aztec lived. Much of their work goes on in the big cities, which were home to Aztec royalty and the main temples. Most Aztec sites are buried beneath modern Mexican cities. Many other sources of information remain for researchers studying the Aztec. Few original Aztec codices survived the conquest. However, many of the records that Sahagún and Durán had Aztec artists re-

ABOVE: *A man dressed in Aztec costume dances during a Christian festival in Mexico City. Descendants of the Aztec often combine Christian and traditional beliefs.*

create are still intact. Archaeologists hope to learn more about the Aztecs as more of these documents are translated and studied.

LEFT: *A descendant of the Aztec takes part in a celebration to mark the arrival of spring.*

The Modern Aztec

The Aztec never completely died out. Today about 1.6 million people in Mexico still speak a dialect, or type, of Nahuatl. In many ways, the lives of the Mexican Indians resemble those of their ancestors. They still grow corn and other crops and eat foods such as tortillas. Although most Mexicans now also have European ancestors, they have come to celebrate the Aztec part of their culture.

While experts work on these translations, more and more archaeologists are now exploring how the Aztec lived outside the centers of the empire. Sites there are often easier to study, because they are not buried by later buildings. Michael E. Smith of Arizona State University has excavated small farm villages in the countryside of Morelos

BELOW: *A young visitor inspects a carved serpent's head in a museum in Mexico City. The Mexican government is encouraging its people to learn about their past.*

state. He has learned that the rural population of the empire grew rapidly in the late 1400s. Farmers had to grow more crops. They began digging terraces and using walls to dam creeks to increase the available land. Soon, however, the population decreased again because the Spanish arrived. Though the Aztec Empire fell, its secrets are again coming to life, thanks to archaeologists.

LEFT: *Felipe Solis Olguin, director of the National Museum of Anthropology in Mexico City, photographed with an Aztec statue. One of Olguin's main concerns is to prevent the stealing of artifacts from Aztec sites (recovered objects, below).*

Further Resources

BOOKS

Clarke, Barry, and Elizabeth Baquedano. *Eyewitness Aztec, Inca, and Maya*. New York: DK Children, 2005.

Cooke, Tim. *National Geographic Investigates Ancient Aztec*. Washington, D.C.: National Geographic, 2008.

Englar, Mary. *Aztec Warriors*. Mankato, MN: Capstone Books, 2008.

Landau, Elaine. *Exploring the World of the Aztecs*. Berkeley Heights, NJ: Enslow Elementary, 2005.

Rees, Rosemary. *The Aztecs* (Understanding People in the Past). Chicago: Heinemann Library, 2006.

WEB SITES

Ancient Scripts site on Aztec writing
http://www.ancientscripts.com/aztec.html

British Museum page on the Aztec
http://www.britishmuseum.org/explore/world_cultures/the_americas/aztecs.aspx

Michael E. Smith's homepage and details of his excavations in Mexico
http://www.public.asu.edu/~mesmith9/

PBS site on the Aztec Empire and its fall
http://www.pbs.org/opb/conquistadors/mexico/mexico.htm

Templo Mayor Museum
http://archaeology.la.asu.edu/tm/index2.php

Glossary

alliance: An agreement between nations to cooperate.

archaeology: The scientific study of cultures by analyzing remains such as artifacts and monuments.

architect: A designer of buildings.

artifact: An object that has been made or changed by humans.

chronicler: Someone who records events as they happen.

city-state: An area ruled by a city.

codex: An illustrated book made by the Aztec or Maya (plural: codices).

conquistador: Spanish for "conqueror."

elite: A group in a society that enjoys special privileges.

empire: A large area of land in which different peoples are ruled by an emperor or empress.

excavation: A scientific dig to explore an archaeological site.

foundation: A base for a building.

glyph: A picture symbol that stands for a specific date, person, or place.

immunity: A natural defense against disease.

myth: A story that explains something important but mysterious, such as how the world was created.

negotiations: Talks between opposed groups.

pyramid: A four-sided structure that rises to a point or a flat top.

ritual: A ceremony carried out as part of religious worship.

sacred: Something worthy of worship.

sacrifice: An offering to the gods, sometimes involving the killing of an animal or a person.

tax: A contribution paid by a citizen to the government for the services provided.

textile: Woven cloth.

tribute: Goods or money paid by one group of people to a stronger one.

Names to Know

Matos Moctezuma, Eduardo (1940–). Mexican archaeologist who has directed excavations at Templo Mayor since 1978.

Smith, Michael E. (1953–). American archaeologist from Arizona State University who excavates rural Aztec sites in Morelos, Mexico.

Index

Page numbers in **bold** type refer
to captions.